Embracing
the
Icon *of* Love

Br. Daniel Korn, CSsR

Liguori

Dedication

I dedicate this book to the School Sisters of Notre Dame,
who instilled in me a great love for the Mother of God, and
in gratitude to those sisters who formed me in my Catholic faith
and introduced me to the Redemptorist brotherhood.

Imprimi Potest:
Stephen T. Rehrauer, CSsR, Provincial
Denver Province, the Redemptorists

Published by Liguori Publications, Liguori, Missouri 63057

To order, visit Liguori.org or call 800-325-9521.

Library of Congress Cataloging-in-Publication Data

Korn, Daniel.
  Embracing the Icon of Love / Daniel Korn, CSsR. — First edition.
    pages cm
  Includes bibliographical references.
  ISBN 978-0-7648-2565-1 (paperback) — ISBN 978-0-7648-7017-0 (eISBN)
  1. Mary, Blessed Virgin, Saint±Meditations. 2. Catholic Church—Doctrines. 3. Love.
  I. Title.
  BT608.5.K67 2015
  232.91—dc23
                                2015005801

Liguori Publications, a nonprofit corporation, is an apostolate of the Redemptorists.
To learn more about the Redemptorists, visit Redemptorists.com.

Printed in the United States of America
19 18 17 16 15 / 5 4 3 2
First Edition

Contents

Preface

W hen I was eight years old, my mother would bring me with her to the Sorrowful Mother Novena every Friday evening. What was unique was that we were not Catholic at the time. This experience of devotion to our Blessed Virgin was instrumental in leading my family to the Church and to a deeper experience of Christ.

I am now a religious brother in the Redemptorist Congregation, founded in 1732 by St. Alphonsus Liguori, a doctor of the Church and a prolific author. Saint Alphonsus had a deep love of Mary. His book *The Glories of Mary* is regarded as his masterpiece.

The constitutions of our religious congregation urge us to take Mary as our model and helper. "For she went on her pilgrim way in faith, and embraced with her whole heart the saving will of God. She dedicated herself completely as a handmaid of the Lord to the person of her Son and to his work, and thus served the mystery of redemption" (Constitution 32).

I quote our constitution because the icon of Our Mother of Perpetual Help is a proclamation of what we as Redemptorists are called to be and do in our preaching: We are called to proclaim the love of God and to lead people to Christ Jesus, the font of plentiful redemption.

One way Redemptorists fulfill this call is by preaching parish missions. Over the past ten years, I have developed a series of missions and novenas centered on the icon of Our Mother of Perpetual Help. Many have asked me to share these materials, so for the first time I present them in book form.

While many readers may be familiar with the traditional devotions to Our Mother of Perpetual Help, my work here promotes the message contained in the iconography. The restoration of the icon in the early 1990s has revealed its deeper meaning and has given us an opportunity to uncover the mysteries contained therein.

Let us invite Mary to be our teacher and model as we enter into the sacred mysteries contained in this miraculous icon.

PART I

Introduction

Chapter 1

What Is an Icon?

The word *icon*, which means "to describe an image," has a long history. It originated in ancient Greece and is still used today, often to describe people or symbols. An internet search of *icon* grants access to a world of possibilities. But in its religious and spiritual context, *icon* is still comparable to its meaning in the modern context.

Iconography, the process of writing and painting icons, involves symbols that reveal messages hidden within a particular image. By gazing on an icon when we're in a contemplative state of prayer, we can read the mystery found within the image. Although people are attracted to the beauty of these images, they often miss the deeper meaning because they're unfamiliar with the practice of reading and praying icons.

Most icons are painted in a style that engages the viewer. The direction of eyes and placement of hands, as well as the colors and symbols around the icon, are fashioned with purpose.

> Icons are not static objects of sacred imagery that remind us of the holy. Rather, they're energy-filled realities that draw us into a relationship with what the image represents.

Icons are windows into mystery. When we look into an icon with faith and devotion, we can feel a sense of being drawn into a living presence. Subjects seem to be looking at us through a window frame. We're summoned into the presence of the active spiritual energy in the image.

Iconography exposes us to the world of the sacred. Gazing with faith upon an icon of Christ, the Virgin, saints, or angels, we experience a sense of presence. Icons are not static objects of sacred imagery that remind us of the holy. They're energy-filled realities that draw us into a relationship with what the image represents.

When we pray and gaze on icons, we're invited to go inward. This engagement with the world of the sacred can change us and form in us a surprising and unexpected response to the world.

Encounters with icons often bring us into a world of active spiritual experiences. They can cause us to experience God in a very different way. Just as modern social and athletic icons inspire us with their accomplishments, sacred icons stir us to recognize the Divine in our midst. But sacred icons are more than inspirational and artful enhancements that uplift our spirits. They are also a gift of a living sacred presence experienced through our sense of sight.

When we focus on sacred images within iconography, we see the mystery of salvation with new eyes of awareness as we're called into a deeper experience of the holy.

In this book, which includes color images, I will explore with you the best-known Marian icon in the world—the icon of Our Mother of Perpetual Help—to help us grow closer to Jesus.

 Questions for Reflection

1. Reflect on your experience of Mary. Do you have a special devotion to Mary? How did you acquire the practice of Marian Prayer?

2. What drew you to pray before Mary? Why do you continue?

3. Gaze a few moments into the icon of Our Mother of Perpetual Help, then ask yourself what thoughts or feelings arose.

Chapter 2

How to Read and Pray With Icons

When we speak of reading and praying with an icon, what do we mean?

Iconography is not understood well in the Latin Church. But the spiritual and theological development of iconography has a long history in the Eastern Churches. We can learn how to read and pray with icons by listening to the words of theologians from the Eastern traditions. For example, the Russian Orthodox theologian Sergius Bulgakov (1871–1944)—in his book *Icons and the Name of God*—describes the icon as "a mode in which this Divine energy radiates into us."

When praying before an icon in faith and devotion, he says, we experience an exchange of energy, a divine presence. "The Divine energy should be understood in a mystically physical sense: the countenance on the icon shines forth, and this radiation enters our spiritual center, our heart, illuminating it."

> When praying before an icon in faith and devotion, we experience an exchange of energy, a divine presence.

In simple terms, our intention to pray and our baptismal life allow us access to the divine presence. This privileged access makes it possible for us to experience what some spiritual writers call the "space of God"—a concept describing God's movement in creation and in our lives.

The concept of God "making a space" is described through the act of his creation:

- God made a space in creating Adam and Eve.
- God made a space in Abraham.
- God made a space in his Chosen People, in Moses, in the camp of Israel, and in the ark.
- God made a space in Mary's womb.
- God makes a space in you, in me, and in all who are baptized.
- We can say that God makes a space in the creation of an icon, too.

In the divine presence spoken of by iconographers, we can say we are in the space of Mary when we gaze upon an icon of Mary. We are also in the space of God that resides within Mary. Those who engage the icon with the full strength of their understanding will find in the icon a means to contemplate the mysteries of Christ.

As we will see in our further reading of the icon of Our Mother of Perpetual Help, the icon is filled with teachings on how to develop interior strength and how to give ourselves to Jesus ever anew, every day.

Questions for Reflection

1. What have you experienced while praying before the icon?

2. Reflect on the quality of your prayer.

3. What are your feelings when you pray?

4. Why do you practice devotion to the Mother of God?

PART II

Praying With the Icon of Our Mother of Perpetual Help

THE FIVE ELEMENTS

Chapter 3

Before You Begin

No other image offers us more possibility of meditation on the heart of the Gospel message than the icon of Our Mother of Perpetual Help. This icon is truly the Gospel in image form. We approach the icon in a spirit of faith and humility. Only those of faith can uncover the hidden messages contained in the image before us.

The Greeks have a word for the type of icon we have in the icon of Our Mother of Perpetual Help, *Hodegetria*, which means, "One who shows the Way." This perfectly describes Mary's role in revealing to us the Gospel message. She stands before us looking intently out to those in front of her with her right hand pointing toward the Child she is holding. Mary, in this icon, is teacher and evangelist. She is a way shower into the mystery of Christ. The Church teaches us that Mary's mission is that of leading others to Christ, and in the icon of Our Mother of Perpetual Help we encounter Mary as the way shower, the sign that proclaims the mystery of Christ to the world.

> Icons are often described as "windows" into the mystery of God. Thus, the image of Our Mother of Perpetual Help invites us into the mystery of Jesus and Mary.

The icon of Our Mother of Perpetual Help presents no written words to be read but rather speaks to us through signs and symbols to be noticed. We use the method called the prayer of gazing to unpack the message contained within these symbols.

The whole image of Our Mother of Perpetual Help is about Jesus Christ and Mary's role as his Mother. When we look at the icon of Our Mother of Perpetual Help, we are invited to read what is contained in the image. We are invited to read the icon as we would read a page in Scripture. This reading of the icon leads us into an experience of Mary that deepens our devotion to her. Through reading the signs and symbols presented in the icon, we are led into a deeper experience of God.

Icons are "windows" into the mystery of God. And this particular icon invites us into the mystery of Jesus and Mary. The icon of Our Mother of Perpetual Help is a sign of the Incarnation as well as the other mysteries in the lives of Jesus and Mary.

In the icon of Our Mother of Perpetual Help, we read five "chapters" or elements of the Gospel story of Jesus.

1. The first chapter is the **Face of the Blessed Mother.**
2. The second chapter is the **Right Hand** that points directly into the heart-center of the Child she is holding.
3. The third chapter is the **Infant God** she presents to us.
4. The fourth chapter is the **Angels**.
5. The fifth chapter is the **Golden Background**.

The prophet Isaiah proclaimed, "Therefore the Lord himself will give you a sign; the young woman, pregnant and about to bear a son, shall name him Emmanuel" (7:14).

This is the Scripture that surrounds the icon of Our Mother of Perpetual Help. Mary is a sign. She cradles a Child. And his name is "God with us!" As we look at the icon, we encounter this prophecy straight on.

Chapter 4

The Face

Images on pages 50-53

The Eight-pointed Star

The first thing many notice in the icon is the eight-pointed star on the top of Mary's veil. This most ancient symbol of Mary comes to us from the catacombs. Ancient artists used the eight-pointed star to identify images of Mary.

> Mary is the star that leads us to redeeming love.

The star of the Magi in the infancy narratives comes to mind as the symbol that captured the imagination of the Roman Christians.

It became a statement connecting Mary with the revelation of the Incarnation as well as a way to identify her image.

Mary, according to St. Bonaventure, is the aurora, the early-morning star that precedes the rising Sun of Justice—Jesus. Mary is the rising star who drives away the night of sin and prepares the way for the mercy and love of God to be manifested in the flesh, Jesus Christ, the Redeemer.

As St. Luke writes in his Gospel, quoting the angel Gabriel "... you will conceive in your womb and bear a son, and you shall name him Jesus. He will be great and will be called Son of the Most High" (1:31–32).

We sing in hymns and antiphons, *"Ave Maris Stella,"* that star of the sea that guides the ships to the shore of safety. Mary is the portal of the sky, the one announcing the coming of the Son of God. She is the star that leads us to redeeming love.

In his apostolic exhortation *Evangelii Gaudium* (2013) Pope Francis states: "She constantly contemplates the mystery of God in our world, in human history and in our daily lives. She is the woman of prayer and work in Nazareth, and she is also Our Lady of Help, who sets out from her town 'with haste' (Luke 1:39) to be of service to others. This interplay of justice and tenderness, of contemplation and concern for others, is what makes the ecclesial community look to Mary as a model of evangelization."

The Eyes of
the Virgin

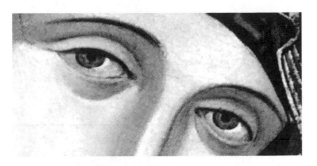

Mary's eyes are often the second element that attracts our attention. They draw you into the icon. Her look is one of great tenderness but also one of intensity.

Her eyes are not directed toward Jesus or toward the activity of the angels, but always facing toward the one who is looking at her.

This is a special effect of Marian icons. Usually when the icon is pictured with Mary and the Child, we are to understand that Jesus is blessing anyone at whom his Mother is gazing upon.

In iconography, the Child Jesus is usually featured with his hand in the form of a blessing while looking at his Mother and holding either a scroll or a Scripture book in his other hand. This is the case in Our Lady of Czestochowa and the well-known icon *Salus Populi Romani,* which is located in St. Mary's Major in Rome. The message of these two icons tells us that whoever Mary gazes upon, Christ the Word incarnate will bless.

In the icon of Our Mother of Perpetual Help, however, the Child is not holding the scroll, nor is he looking at his Mother or those before the icon. His energy is trained toward the angel with the cross. His expression reflects the same intensity as his Mother's.

Both the looks of Mary and of Jesus portray a sense of pondering and contemplation at the events surrounding them. Both faces convey they are listening reflectively. The iconographers show us the ear of Mary and the ear of the child, exposed, inviting us to notice this detail. These exposed ears teach us an attitude of contemplative listening to the movement of God in our lives and the importance of cultivating it.

The Virgin, who listens to the word of the angel, and the Child *Logos* are always attuned to the will of the Father. The Virgin's eyes look out to us, and the eyes of the Child look to the cross.

The Ears and Mouth of the Virgin

We notice, too, the smallness of Mary's mouth and that her right ear is exposed from under her veil. These elements teach us that in order to hear the voice of God, we must be silent and listen.

The exposed ear and smallness of the mouth are the way the iconographer presents the ancient teaching of the annunciation experience. Mary listened to the voice of the angel and she accepted her role to be the Mother of the Redeemer.

The first lesson of reading the icon is to create space in our daily lives for the action of God. Mary's example of listening and her attentiveness to the moments of God are her lessons to us of the importance of being quiet and listening. We are to follow Mary's attitude in our own lives, making sure that we allow for time to be silent in the presence of God.

MAY MARY, OUR MOTHER OF PERPETUAL HELP, OBTAIN FOR US THE GRACE TO IMITATE HER IN OUR AWARENESS OF THE MOVEMENT OF GOD THAT SURROUNDS OUR DAILY EXPERIENCES.

John 2:1–11: The Wedding at Cana

On the third day there was a wedding in Cana in Galilee, and the mother of Jesus was there. Jesus and his disciples were also invited to the wedding. When the wine ran short, the mother of Jesus said to him, "They have no wine." [And] Jesus said to her, "Woman, how does your concern affect me? My hour has not yet come." His mother said to the servers, "Do whatever he tells you." Now there were six stone water jars there for Jewish ceremonial washings, each holding twenty to thirty gallons. Jesus told them, "Fill the jars with water." So they filled them to the brim. Then he told them, "Draw some out now and take it to the headwaiter." So they took it. And when the headwaiter tasted the water that had become wine, without knowing where it came from (although the servers who had drawn the water knew), the headwaiter called the bridegroom and said to him, "Everyone serves good wine first, and then when people have drunk freely, an inferior one; but you have kept the good wine until now." Jesus did this as the beginning of his signs in Cana in Galilee and so revealed his glory, and his disciples began to believe in him.

John's Gospel story begins with the invitation Mary, Jesus, and the disciples receive to attend the celebration. Through the intense look of the eyes in the icon of Our Mother of Perpetual Help, we are invited to celebrate with her the marriage feast of the Incarnation: Jesus, God's Son, taking on our human condition.

The Gospel continues with Mary's statement to Jesus that "they have no wine." Mary's eyes take in the problem; she responds to the need by bringing it to Jesus' attention. Mary preannounces the kingdom to Jesus in asking him to act with the miracle of turning the water into wine.

Questions for Reflection

1. Reading the icon of Our Mother of Perpetual Help begins with reflection on Mary's face. What part of the reading of her face touches you?

2. As you pray the icon, slowing with attention, how do you experience what the icon teaches in the symbols of the elements of Mary's face?

3. What does reading and praying the icon do for you?

Chapter 5

The Hands of Mary

Images on pages 54–55

I n the icon we see the right hand of Mary pointing to the image of the Christ. It is not grasping the hand of the Infant, which would be the natural pose and response of a mother whose child had

> As we look into the mystery, now we become the ones who must extend our hands and receive this Word, this Christ made flesh.

just placed his hand in hers. Mary's hand is straight and pointing to what she is holding in her arms, which is the Christ.

The position of the Virgin in this icon is of one standing and presenting the Infant to the one who is looking on the icon. Notice her left hand and arm. She is not holding the Infant to herself: rather, it is as if she is presenting the Infant to the one who stands before the icon: you and me.

We are invited to respond to this presentation by becoming the ones who must extend our hands and receive this Word, this Christ made flesh. It is as if she is saying to us, "Receive this Word of your salvation!" Mary is inviting us to renew our commitment to live the Gospel and proclaim Christ through our words and actions.

Also notice that the right hand of Mary is straight and pointing directly into the heart center of the Child. If we were to take a ruler and place it on the tip of the middle finger of Mary's right hand, we would be able to draw a line directly through the Infant up to the cross the angel is holding. This visual line informs us that this is no ordinary little baby. With this gesture, Mary is proclaiming the paschal mystery.

This pointing hand tells us much, but it must always be seen and read in the context of what has been read in the face of the Virgin. The face of the Virgin is about her eyes, ear, and mouth; all these elements call us to enter into a space of contemplation. This is what happens when we come before her and our eyes connect with hers.

Pope St. John Paul II, in his apostolic letter *Rosarium Virginis Mariae,* has a section titled "Mary, Model of Contemplation," which says:

The contemplation of Christ has an incomparable model in Mary.

In a unique way the face of the Son belongs to Mary. It was in her womb that Christ was formed, receiving from her a human resemblance, which points to an even greater spiritual closeness.

No one has ever devoted himself to the contemplation of "the face of Christ as faithfully as Mary."

When at last she gave birth to Him in Bethlehem, her eyes were able to gaze tenderly on the face of her Son, as she "wrapped Him in swaddling clothes, and laid Him in a manger" (Luke 2:7).

In the section "Mary's Memories," St. John Paul II continues:

> Mary lived with her eyes fixed on Christ, treasuring His every word; "She kept all these things, pondering them in her heart" (Luke 2:19; see 2:51). The memories of Jesus, impressed upon her heart, were always with her, leading her to reflect on the various moments of her life at her Son's side.

The image of our Lady before us is an image of a woman who has pondered and contemplated Jesus.

In the Scripture story of the Presentation, Mary stands before us in the pondering stance that St. Luke speaks of twice in his account of the infancy narrative.

"And Mary kept all these things, reflecting on them in her heart" (Luke 2:19), and later in verse 51 "[…] and his mother kept all these things in her heart."

What is this pondering of Mary? It is more than just a recalling of past events. The Greek word used in the Scripture is translated as "piecing together." For Mary, pondering is like contemplating and meditating on all the events that have happened in her life concerning Jesus. She sees into the deeper, inner meaning of everything happening around her.

This is the contemplation of Mary. It is what she is teaching us to do in our lives. The look on her face in the icon reflects this meaning of pondering and remembering.

Scriptural Reflection

Luke 2:22–35: The Presentation in the Temple

When the days were completed for their purification according to the law of Moses, they took him up to Jerusalem to present him to the Lord, just as it is written in the law of the Lord, "Every male that opens the womb shall be consecrated to the Lord," and to offer the sacrifice of "a pair of turtledoves or two young pigeons," in accordance with the dictate in the law of the Lord.

Now there was a man in Jerusalem whose name was Simeon. This man was righteous and devout, awaiting the consolation of Israel, and the holy Spirit was upon him. It had been revealed to him by the holy Spirit that he should not see death before he had seen the Messiah of the Lord. He came in the Spirit into the temple; and when the parents brought in the child Jesus to perform the custom of the law in regard to him, he took him into his arms and blessed God, saying:

"Now, Master, you may let your servant go in peace, according to your word, for my eyes have seen your salvation, which you prepared in sight of all the peoples, a light for revelation to the Gentiles, and glory for your people Israel."

The child's father and mother were amazed at what was said about him; and Simeon blessed them and said to Mary his mother, "Behold, this child is destined for the fall and rise of many in Israel, and to be a sign that will be contradicted (and you yourself a sword will pierce) so that the thoughts of many hearts may be revealed."

This Gospel story is filled with the movements of the hand. Mary and Joseph present the Child to the aged Simeon. He takes the Child and offers him to God and then gives the Child back to the Mother, giving the prophecy:

"(And you yourself a sword will pierce) so that the thoughts of many hearts may be revealed."

This is a familiar story to us. Our prayer books and churches are filled with art that depicts this scene. We should have no problem picturing it.

Simeon's prophecy about the sword that will pierce the heart of Mary is about her and the role she will play in the salvation of the world. At the same time, in this icon, it is about us.

When Simeon says "that the thoughts of many hearts may be revealed," he is talking about Mary's role in teaching us and leading all those who would take up the gospel life.

May we enter this world of Mary's remembering in our thoughts and in our reflections, in our ponderings and in our contemplation.

Questions for Reflection

1. Do you ponder the events in your life, taking time to remember the many ways God has affected your life story?

2. As you continue to read and pray the icon, ask Mary to be present with you in the examination of your life. Ask her to help you see with eyes of faith the messages God is revealing in your experiences.

3. Meditate on the words of Simeon to Mary: "(And you yourself a sword will pierce) so that the thoughts of many hearts may be revealed." What are your many thoughts at this moment?

Chapter 6

The Child *(Logos)*

Images on pages 56–59

There is much here that deserves our prayerful attention. Let us look at this Child and reflect on what our eyes take in. Bear in mind that this image is that of Jesus as God-man. We now read of his divinity and humanity in the mystery of the Incarnation.

Mary invites us and teaches us to embrace this Infant and take into ourselves the incarnate-crucified mystery of Redemption.

The Gaze of the Child

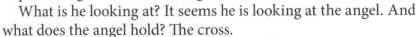

We can see the look on the face of
Jesus. He imitates his Mother's look
of pondering and remembering.

What is he looking at? It seems he is looking at the angel. And
what does the angel hold? The cross.

In this vision, Jesus is pulled into wonder. His look is not of
fear but of prayerful pondering and contemplation. As with his
Mother's pondering and contemplation, he is piecing together the
vision of the angels appearing before him in his vision dream.

He is totally taken up into this vision, not looking at his Mother
or at us: He is focused on the cross, teaching us to reflect upon the
passion of Jesus.

The Garments of the Child

The green color of his tunic illustrates that Jesus is fully human. "One
like us in all things except sin," as we
pray in the Eucharistic Prayer. The red
cincture indicates that all humanity
and all creation has been wrapped in
redemptive love. The golden-brown
overlay cloaking the rest of his body
is filled with the "Golden Light" of
the resurrection.

The Feet of the
Child *Logos*

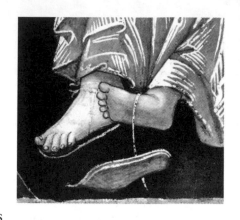

Next we look at his left foot. It
seems somewhat contorted and
twisted, as if it hurts. This is a
dual symbol the iconographer has
placed in the image. It symbolizes his crucified body and Genesis
3:15: "I will put enmity between you and the woman, and between
your offspring and hers; They will strike at your head, while you
strike at their heel."

This symbol of the foot turned up to show its sole and heel says
he is the one who will crush the serpent. He will crush and destroy
the grip of evil in the three days of the passion of the Lord.

The Form of the Body of the Child *Logos*
The iconographer has imprinted another element of the passion in
the shape of the Child's body through the way his legs are crossed
under his garments. It is a very slight emphasis, but if you look with
attention at the folds of the garment you can see the imprint of the
crossed legs. The manner in which one foot is longer than the other
is another statement of the crucifixion. On images of the crucified
Christ we notice one foot pulled longer and placed over the other
and nailed to the wood of the cross.

The Falling Sandal of the Child
The falling sandal is a sign of Jesus' humility in taking on our humanity. "Though he was in the form of God, did not regard equality with
God something to be grasped. Rather, he emptied himself, taking
the form of a slave, coming in human likeness; and found human in
appearance" (Philippians 2:6-7). He conceals his divine nature in his
humanity and lets fall the Golden Sandal, the symbol of his glory.

In this presentation of the Infant Christ, we are being invited into a dialogue about the mystery of redemption: the Incarnation, passion, death, and resurrection.

As Mary is pointing to the Christ and we take in the vision of Jesus, we are being instructed by her to embrace the passion of Jesus within our own hearts as if she is saying: "receive the Mystery of Redemption."

Scriptural Reflection
Luke 2:41–52: The Boy Jesus in the Temple

Each year his parents went to Jerusalem for the feast of Passover, and when he was twelve years old, they went up according to festival custom. After they had completed its days, as they were returning, the boy Jesus remained behind in Jerusalem, but his parents did not know it. Thinking that he was in the caravan, they journeyed for a day and looked for him among their relatives and acquaintances, but not finding him, they returned to Jerusalem to look for him. After three days they found him in the temple, sitting in the midst of the teachers, listening to them and asking them questions, and all who heard him were astounded at his understanding and his answers. When his parents saw him, they were astonished, and his mother said to him, "Son, why have you done this to us? Your father and I have been looking for you with great anxiety." And he said to them, "Why were you looking for me? Did you not know that I must be in my Father's house?" But they did not understand what he said to them. He went down with them and came to Nazareth, and was obedient to them; and his mother kept all these things in her heart. And Jesus advanced [in] wisdom and age and favor before God and man.

This Gospel account is the familiar story of Mary and Joseph searching for Jesus after leaving Jerusalem.

What are some of the images (icons) that form in our minds when we ponder this story (imitating Mary's pondering) in our hearts?

Mary and Joseph notice Jesus is missing after three days, which might seem strange to us. Going up to Jerusalem is, in itself, symbolic in biblical writings. For Jesus it is the place where he proclaims who he is. Many of the teachings about the kingdom of God take place when Jesus is in Jerusalem, and Jerusalem is the place of the passion, death, and resurrection of the Christ.

Scripture says that, according to the custom, they went up for the feast. Luke tells us they did not know Jesus, age twelve, was missing. It is possible they went up to the Temple one last time, and the custom was to leave in separate groups and catch up with each other later in the journey. There are many ancient documents with opinions on this Scripture passage, but we can only speculate, based on the varied commentaries and historical sources, how Jesus may have come to be separated from Joseph and Mary on this three-day trek.

Mary and Joseph, full of anxiety, search for Jesus everywhere. Spiritual writers conclude this to be symbolic of our searching for the holy in our own lives. It is a thought worthy of reflecting upon.

This anxious searching reminded Mary of the prophecy of old Simeon about the sword that would strike her heart. Simeon's words to her of the Child being "destined for the falling and the rising of many in Israel" were certainly on her mind in this moment. All this was part of the pondering and piecing together of the memories of Jesus in her life. Only parents who have temporarily lost a child in a crowd can relate to this anxiety.

In retracing their steps, they find their way to the Temple and find Jesus talking with doctors and elders. Jewish tradition even today retains a custom of young men engaging the learned rabbis in discussion of the Torah. This is the setting Luke presents.

As we reflect on this story, we are presented with many questions. The dialogue of Mary with Jesus leaves us somewhat confused. "Son, why have you done this to us? Your father and I have been looking for you with great anxiety" (Luke 2:48).

In relation to the icon of Our Mother of Perpetual Help, the application is clear. In this exchange of Jesus with Mary, we observe the ages-old tradition of devotion to Mary. We see in her one who understands our anxious questioning. We go to her in prayer asking for her maternal help. This is an important element of the tradition of the many novenas to Our Mother of Perpetual Help.

Like Mary and Joseph, we are on a journey, a pilgrimage searching for Christ. We come before this icon, read it, and pray it to connect to the mystery of Christ in a deeper way. Mary invites and teaches us to embrace this Infant and take into ourselves the incarnate-crucified mystery of Redemption.

Mary teaches us how to be open to Christ, the Word of God, and she desires to form Jesus in us, to help us be transformed in the image of Jesus, to be Jesus for others, this day.

Like Mary and Joseph in the story of the seeming loss of the Child Jesus in the Scripture, we are on a journey searching for the mystery of Christ. In returning to Jerusalem, Mary and Joseph had to find the lost Jesus in his role as Savior. This returning to Jerusalem is symbolic of finding within ourselves the inner temple—Christ's mystical presence—which we received at baptism.

I invite you to spend time gazing on this Infant. Allow the image into your mind's eye and simply hold it there in silence.

Questions for Reflection

1. As you gaze on the icon after hearing the explanation of the symbols contained in the Child, what symbol attracts you most?

2. Now that you know of the many elements of the passion of Jesus contained within the image of Child *Logos*, what do the Incarnation, passion, death, and resurrection mean to you?

3. How is the passion of Jesus present in your daily living? What does it mean for you to be living the Gospel in your daily life? Does meditation on the passion of Jesus open you to compassion? Are there places in your life that need to be healed?

Chapter 7

The Angels

Images on pages 60–63

Angels present instruments of the passion to Christ. They carry them in veiled hands, thus announcing the message of the dignity of the glorified, crucified, and resurrected Jesus. The passion proclaims the redemptive love of God for us in Christ—the mystery of Jesus in Mary and Mary in Jesus. The icon of Our Mother of Perpetual Help initiates the reality of the Father's great love for humanity.

> Through the Incarnation, passion, and resurrection of the Lord, we receive copious redemption. This is the central message of the icon.

Through the Incarnation, passion, and resurrection of the Lord, we receive copious redemption. This is the central message of the iconography in the icon of Our Mother of Our Perpetual Help.

The passion is for us the gate of glory, as our Lord told the disciples on the way to Emmaus. "Was it not necessary that the Messiah should suffer these things and enter into his glory?" (Luke 24:26).

If we suffer with Jesus and Mary we shall also be glorified with them. "The Spirit itself bears witness with our spirit that we are children of God, and if children, then heirs, heirs of God and joint heirs with Christ, if only we suffer with him so that we may also be glorified with him" (Romans 8:16–17).

The Archangel Gabriel

The archangel Gabriel is on the right as we face the icon. The Greek letters "OAP" above the angel on the right as we face the icon tell us this is Gabriel. Another way we know this is Gabriel is that in Christian tradition, Gabriel is considered Mary's guardian angel, being the one chosen to visit her at the annunciation.

In the icon, this angel is on the same physical level as Mary. If she turned her gaze to the left, she would see Gabriel. The angel slightly bows toward her and she bows slightly to the angel, revealing the actions that took place during the annunciation.

Gabriel holds in his hands the cross and nails of the passion of Christ and seems to be engaging the attention of the Child-*Logos*.

Notice that the angel holds these instruments of the terrible sufferings of Jesus with a cloth, with veiled hands—a sign of reverence and respect.

Veiling sacred objects is a longstanding liturgical rubric. Altar cloths, the cloth used to wipe the chalice during Communion, and the humeral veil used in the benediction all reflect our respect and reverence.

The passion of Jesus is only implied in the angels. We do not see in this icon the crucifixion itself nor the resurrection. The sacred cloths depicted in the icon show reverence and respect for the connectedness of the realities of the glorified, crucified, and resurrected Christ.

The Archangel Michael

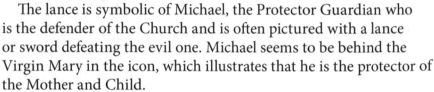

The archangel Michael is on the left as you face the icon. The Greek letters "OAPM" tell us this is Michael.

Michael's sleeve stripes tell us he is an archangel of high rank. He holds in his veiled hands the lance, sponge, and the jar of gall and vinegar, all of which will be used in the crucifixion.

The lance is symbolic of Michael, the Protector Guardian who is the defender of the Church and is often pictured with a lance or sword defeating the evil one. Michael seems to be behind the Virgin Mary in the icon, which illustrates that he is the protector of the Mother and Child.

The instruments held by the two angels, combined with the *Theotokos*—the Mother of God—and the figure of Christ, explicitly evoke the mystery of the Incarnation, passion, death, and resurrection of Christ. The icon is, in miniature, the story of our full redemption. It is presented as a symbol of God's saving love.

The instruments of Jesus already have the sacred value conferred on them by their association with these mysteries. These instruments of the passion are not signs of defeat but are presented as the means of Jesus' universality of salvation by means of the cross.

That is why there is a "flow of energy" from the face of the Virgin through her right hand into the Christ up to the angel he is gazing upon. And everything is penetrated by the divine light we see in the golden glow of the icon.

Acts 1:12–14 and 2:1–4: Pentecost

Then they returned to Jerusalem from the mount called Olivet, which is near Jerusalem, a sabbath day's journey away. When they entered the city they went to the upper room where they were staying, Peter and John and James and Andrew, Philip and Thomas, Bartholomew and Matthew, James son of Alphaeus, Simon the Zealot, and Judas son of James. All these devoted themselves with one accord to prayer, together with some women, and Mary the mother of Jesus, and his brothers.

[....]When the time for Pentecost was fulfilled, they were all in one place together. And suddenly there came from the sky a noise like a strong driving wind, and it filled the entire house in which they were. Then there appeared to them tongues as of fire, which parted and came to rest on each one of them. And they were all filled with the holy Spirit and began to speak in different tongues, as the Spirit enabled them to proclaim.

This Scripture, the familiar story of Pentecost, is important in helping us uncover the meaning of the icon.

Regarding Mary, it is significant because we see her in the role of Mother of the Church. "In the primitive Church she is seen praying with the apostles, in our own day she is actively present, and the Church desires to live the mystery of Christ with her: 'grant that your church which with Mary shared Christ's passion may be worthy to share also in his resurrection.'" Mary is in the midst of the disciples, praying and awaiting the coming of the Holy Spirit (quotation from *Marialis Cultus*, apostolic exhortation of Blessed Pope Paul VI, 1974).

Mary in the midst of the Church is the Mother of the Church. She sits amidst the apostles, the teachers who would bring the Good News of salvation to the world. She teaches the inner meaning of the Pentecost story. She teaches us devoted prayer and, by her body language, a pondering kind of silence. Her lessons teach us to contemplate the Gospel message.

In the icon of Our Mother of Perpetual Help, Mary is in our midst now. She draws us in through her eyes and points to the subject of our pondering and contemplating: the Infant Christ and all he symbolizes. Following Christ's pondering gaze, we are drawn into the angels and what they represent in this icon.

Questions for Reflection

1. As you center your attention on the two angels in the icon, what thoughts come to you as you reflect on the instruments of the passion they hold?

2. The angels give a hint of the glory (resurrection) of Jesus as they hold the instruments of the passion in veiled hands. How do you experience the suffering and pains of life all around you as well as the glorious news of the resurrection?

3. Angels are messengers of God. In this icon they seem to present to us the mystery of salvation, the Incarnation, passion, death, and resurrection of Jesus. Reflect on how you are living the mystery of Christ in your daily life. What do the following words of St. Paul inspire in you? "May I never boast of anything but the cross of our Lord Jesus Christ...for I bear the marks of Jesus on my body" (Galatians 6:14, 17).

The Golden Background

Image on page 64

The icon of Our Mother of Perpetual Help represents the mystery of salvation in Christ. The gilded background of the icon (also called the purest light) and circular halos invite us to contemplate Christ and the Mother of God already living the full glory of the great mystery of the Redemption.

> The final experience of the icon is the most powerful. The gold light that surrounds the image also comes forth through the image. It is the divine light of God.

Jesus' saving action at the Incarnation through the elevation on the cross and his ascent into heaven on the day of the resurrection all comprise this mystery of Redemption. Raised on the cross, he appears to all as the Savior of the world. Exalted at the right hand of the Father, in glory, he will send forth the Holy Spirit who—through him—will extend his dominion in the world.

We proclaim in the Eucharistic Prayer: "Save us Savior of the world, for by your cross and resurrection you have set us free." This brings us back to the first chapter of this book, where we began the journey to experience the power and grace of this icon.

The message is that of the Gospel. We are gazing into the heart of the Gospel as we reflect on each of the elements of the icon and the windows into the mystery it represents.

It is this that makes the icon of Our Mother of Perpetual Help a world of symbols and messages. At the same time, it is an inexhaustible source of aesthetic and religious contemplation. It is not surprising, therefore, that in contemplation of this icon one should move easily from artistic admiration to authentic Christian prayer, the purpose for which it was created.

The final experience of the icon is the most powerful.

The same golden light of the background radiates throughout the icon, highlighting the divine light of God. The gold highlights on the garments are not just for accent. It is the healing, compassionate light of the Godhead, the same light that infused the body of Jesus at the resurrection. It is same light by which Jesus said: "I am the Light of the world."

This light is coming into you and it is because of this that the icon is considered a "miraculous" one through which great healing and reconciliation happen.

Stand before this icon and breathe in this divine light, read the elements that present themselves to you, and allow the holy presence of God to embrace you.

Mary will provide this for all who come before her icon with humility and faith. She will form Jesus in us. This is her mission.

What was from the beginning,
what we have heard,
what we have seen with our eyes,
what we looked upon
and touched with our hands
concerns the Word of life—
for the life was made visible;
we have seen it and testify to it
and proclaim to you the eternal life
that was with the Father and was made visible to us—
what we have seen and heard
we proclaim now to you,
so that you too may have fellowship with us;
for our fellowship is with the Father
and with his Son, Jesus Christ.
We are writing this so that our joy may be complete.

This is the message we have heard from him and proclaim to you: God is light, and in him there is no darkness. If we say, "We have fellowship with him," to paraphrase 1 John, while we continue to walk in darkness, we do not act in truth.

This Scripture speaks to us as we read the last element, the gold that is so prominent in the icon and is symbolic of the light John speaks about in this reading.

All of the reflection we have done while reading and praying the icon is summed up in this Letter of John. Our eyes have been the main instrument we used to gaze and pray. We have contemplated each element of the icon with faith as we come to the last element, the gold, symbolic of the fullness of redemptive love. John continues by saying: "We have fellowship with one another, and the blood of his Son Jesus cleanses us from all sin."

Through praying and reading this icon we experience the meaning of the old Christian hymn: "I've been redeemed by the blood of the Lamb, filled with the Holy Ghost I am. All my sins are washed away, I've been redeemed."

Mary has led us through the mystery of the redemptive love of Jesus Christ. In this icon we have contemplated her teachings of silence and evangelic contemplation of the Incarnation, passion, death, and resurrection.

We can place in her mouth the words from 1 John: "We declare to you what was from the beginning what we have heard, what we have seen with our eyes, what we have looked upon and touched with our hands...the Word of life."

Now we allow the last element of the iconography, the gold, to shine out into us as we stand before the icon in sincere faith. We are invaded by this divine light of Christ and transformed into that which we have contemplated. "We declare what we have seen and heard," as John proclaims. We now become living icons of the redeeming love of Jesus Christ. This is truly "incarnate" prayer. This is transformation into the Living Mystery of Redemption.

Jesus, living in Mary come and live in us for the glory of the Father. Amen.

Questions for Reflection

1. When you pray before the icon, what do you notice about the quality of your prayer? Does reading the icon help you center yourself for contemplative prayer?

2. As you gaze upon the icon, take in the golden color and allow it to surround you in reverent silence.

3. Stay in the space of silence for a certain amount of time. Then gradually come back to activity by praying a Hail Mary slowly.

Chapter 9

The Mystical Consciousness of the Icon

When we talk about the mystical dimension of the icon we refer to the miraculous quality of the image in the spirituality and theology of iconography. The power of an icon lies in the sacred presence it invites us into as we pray and read the image before us.

When we place ourselves before an icon in an attitude of prayer and reflection, we are invited into a spiritual space of divine energy. The face of our Mother of Perpetual Help has this effect on those who pray before her. Her penetrating gaze tends to pull us into the sacred space as she invites us to delve deeply into the mystery of the living Christ.

This icon presents the mystery of Jesus' Incarnation, passion, death, and resurrection and the effects these mysteries have on us. In this way, the icon vibrates with divine energy.

> This icon presents the mystery of Jesus' Incarnation, passion, death, and resurrection and the effects these mysteries have on us.

People with a strong devotion to Mary through this icon have had many powerful experiences, including cures and answered prayers. These events help show the icon's mystical qualities.

It is through these experiences that the title "miraculous" was attached to this icon during the many years it was in Rome in the Church of St. Matthew down to the present day. Its official title is *the Miraculous Icon of Our Mother of Perpetual Help*. What makes an icon "miraculous" is the veneration bestowed upon the image by the faith and devotion of the community.

Thus the icon is more than a picture or image used for religious decoration. Rather, it not only inspires spiritual thoughts and feelings but also engages all who look upon her.

The icon is an efficacious sign of a real presence because it is a sacramental. Icons become a great means of holiness because of the ritual of blessing and the veneration of the image. This allows for the experience of the miraculous interventions and favors bestowed upon those who pray in the presence of an icon.

This icon is also one of intense spirituality because Mary draws our attention to the one she is holding. This icon is about the mystery of Christ in our midst.

Saint Paul, in his Letter to the Colossians, describes the definition of the word *icon*. "He is the image of the invisible God, the firstborn of all creation. For in him were created all things in heaven and on earth, the visible and the invisible, whether thrones or dominions or principalities or powers; all things were created through him and for him" (1:15–16).

It is because of the Incarnation of the Word of God that we can *image* Christ. We have a recorded image of his life among us in the Scriptures.

An image of what some believe to be Jesus is also on the shroud of Turin. This image of the imprint of what may be the face and body of Christ is held in high regard in the Church and is the starting place for many paintings of the image of the Savior.

The manner in which the shroud was folded and displayed for public veneration presented the face of the shroud to viewers and became the first icon of the face of Christ, known by the Christians of the East as the *Holy Mandylion* (an image not made by hands).

The tradition of painting the image of Christ and of the Virgin has a long history in Christian theology and art. The discipline of iconography continues to be one of the ways in which images of Jesus and Mary are created for us today.

In the liturgy of the Byzantine Akathist hymn to the Mother of God, we pray, in the words of Servant of God Fr. Roman Bachtalowsky, CSsR:

> Mother of God, the power of the most High God manifests itself in every place where your precious icon is devoutly honored. *Here the sick regain their health, the suffering receive comfort, and those who dwell in darkness obtain the spiritual sight of the soul and body,* for you attract all with your goodness that you may lead them to your heart and thus turn them toward Christ, the never-setting Sun (*Kondak 3*, emphasis author's).

It is through the miraculous that we engage the mystical consciousness of this great icon of the Mother of God.

The central message of the icon is one of the redeeming love of Jesus Christ. Her icon presence invites us into the mystery of the Incarnation, passion, death, and resurrection of Christ. It is a journey into the depth of the mystery of our salvation in Christ. To those who approach this holy icon with faith and devotion, the possibility of the miraculous becomes open to them. Their devotion to the Mother of God is raised to a level beyond the ordinary experience of piety. It is in this space of devotion that the icon becomes the vehicle for God's presence to the one in prayer before it. For it is said about an icon that it is a place to encounter God.

When one is in this spiritualized space of divine energy, the mystical consciousness of the icon of the Mother of God of Perpetual Help (as she is called in the Eastern rite) unfolds the experience of the miraculous.

It is the fulfillment of the Akathist hymn: "God (is manifested) in every place where your icon is *devoutly honored.*"

The power of the miraculous contained in the icon of Our Mother of Perpetual Help is established through the many ancient liturgical texts contained in the prayers for feasts and solemnities of the Mother of God that the Church celebrates.

The Symbolism of the Image of Mary

As noted earlier, Blessed Pope Paul VI wrote an important apostolic exhortation about "the right ordering and development of devotion to the Blessed Virgin Mary," *Marialis Cultus.*

Paul VI sums up an important element about the Christological orientation of devotion to the Blessed Virgin Mary. The Fathers of the Church attributed to the work of the Spirit the original holiness of Mary, "who was fashioned by the Holy Spirit into a kind of new substance and new creature," the pope writes.

Paul VI draws our attention to the Gospel texts: "The Holy Spirit will come upon you and the power of the Most High will cover you with his shadow" (Luke 1:35). Through this action of the Holy Spirit, the Fathers carved out titles that present to us a further image of the place of the Virgin in the mystery of Christ.

They call Mary the Abode of the King, the Tabernacle of the Lord, the Ark of the Covenant, and the Temple of the Holy Spirit. These are rich titles from the Scriptures that are prototypes of the image of Mary in the mystery of Christ.

Paul VI called us to return to the biblical, patristic, and liturgical emphasis of Mary in the life of the Church. Rooted in these sources, we have before us a way of talking about Mary in her relationship with Christ and the Church.

Iconographers have written into icons these biblical concepts from the Old and New Testaments to show that God prepared a place for the Incarnation of the Word in the womb of Mary.

A theme unique to the icon of Our Mother of Perpetual Help is that of the Ark of the Covenant, a title printed in the Litany of the Blessed Virgin Mary: "Ark of the Covenant, pray for us."

This tradition of seeing Mary as the "new" Ark of the Covenant has its sources in the ancient writings of the Fathers of the Church about the sacredness of Mary's womb as the dwelling place of the Son. Her womb is like that of the ark, in which the holy of holies was contained. In Mary dwelt the incarnate Word of God.

These patristic writings and commentaries are filled with texts on the place of Mary in the life of Christ. The Church, through these scriptural images of the ark and its importance to Israel, mirror the veneration due to Mary as the Mother of God.

A Marian hymn sums up early understanding of her:

The Word whom earth and sea and sky
adore and laud and magnify,
whose might they show, whose praise they tell,
in Mary's body deigned to dwell.

How blessed that Mother, in whose shrine
the world's Creator, Lord divine,
whose hand contains the earth and sky,
once deigned, as in his ark, to lie.

VANANTIUS FORTUNATUS, 530–609

The Word in Mary's womb holds the same honor as the ark. Look carefully at the icon of Our Mother of Perpetual Help to see its symmetry to the description of the ark.

The ark was the "mercy seat" of God, as recorded in Exodus. It was located at the top of the ark, reverenced by two angels facing each other and bowing toward the space of the platform that was understood to be the throne of God's glory.

In the descriptions written in Exodus about the building of the ark, we can see a hint of Mary's place in salvation history. All that was said about the ark could be said about the womb of the Virgin Mary. It was a sacred space in which God would dwell.

Great hymns and canticles would be written about Mary, illuminating this importance. "Rejoice, ark made golden by the Spirit. Rejoice, O Tablet of God's mercy. Rejoice, O Manna sweeter than honey, Rejoice, O Lamp Stand of seven branches that enlightens all!" These evocations describe the central artifacts of the Temple, where God dwelled. This was the sacred space of the Tent of Meeting and eventually of the Temple itself. These acclamations can be said about Mary because she conceived the Son of God through the Holy Spirit.

Many early-Church writers, reflecting on the infancy narratives of the Gospel, praise the incarnate Word borne in the womb of Mary, the prototype of the Old Testament presence of God carried in the Ark of the Covenant.

The Symmetry of the Icon of Our Mother of Perpetual Help

As we look at the icon of Our Mother of Perpetual Help and place ourselves in a space of prayer before the icon, we become aware that we are before something that is filled with holiness and are drawn into God's presence through the eyes of Mary as she looks at us.

If we were to create a line from the tip of the left shoulder of Mary up over the tip of the angel's wings on the left, continue our line across Mary's halo to the tip of the angel's wing on the right, and finally bring our line down the Child's back we would have the same "mercy seat" as in the Ark of the Covenant.

Within this space is present the image of the Christ Child, the Word made flesh, the presence of God, the "mercy seat" of God central to Christian theology. Imaging Mary as the ark invites us to enter into contemplative prayer.

How to Engage the Miraculous Dimension of the Icon

The process of unlocking the miraculous dimension of the icon is discovered through contemplative prayer. Through the prayer practice of "gazing," we enable ourselves to step from our regular routine and place ourselves in a posture of silent prayer.

Icons are created to give us the opportunity to enter into the space of the holy. Mary's gaze draws us into the icon, enabling us to give ourselves to the divine energy contained therein. It is in this space we encounter the miraculous experience of the icon of Our Mother of Perpetual Help. The way into the miraculous space of the icon of Our Mother of Perpetual Help is through the prayer of gazing.

> THE EYE WITH WHICH I SEE GOD IS
> THE SAME EYE WITH WHICH GOD SEES ME.
>
> MEISTER ECKHART, OP

The Icon of Love

The Eight-pointed Star

See page 17

The Eyes of the Virgin

See page 19

The Mouth of the Virgin

See page 20

The Ear of the Virgin

See page 20

The Right Hand of Mary

See page 23

The Right Hand of Mary

See page 23

The Gaze of the Child

See page 29

The Gaze of the Child

See page 29

The Garments of the Child

See page 29

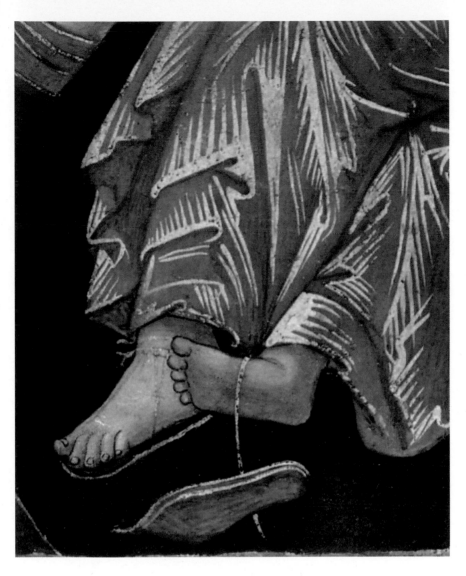

The Falling Sandal of the Child

See page 30

The Archangel Gabriel

See page 35

OAP Above the Archangel Gabriel

See page 35

The Archangel Michael

See page 36

OAPM Above the Archangel Michael

See page 36

The Golden Background

See page 39

Chapter 10

Mary in the Life of the Church Today

T he final chapter of the Dogmatic Constitution on the Church, *Lumen Gentium,* speaks of the place of the Blessed Virgin Mary, Mother of God, in the mysteries of Christ and the Church.

"The Virgin Mary, who at the message of the angel received the Word of God in her heart and in her body and gave Life to the world, is acknowledged and honored as being truly the Mother of God and Mother of the Redeemer" (*LG* 53).

Devotion to Our Mother of Perpetual Help is always understood in the light of this statement. In the iconography we experience Mary as the one who gave her *fiat* through the angel Gabriel and accepted her role as the Mother of the Redeemer she holds.

The star on her veil and her hand pointing to the Christ Child she holds define the message of this icon. She leads us to Christ.

This icon continues to present themes of Mary found in the Scriptures and tradition. We read in this icon signs and symbols taken from the Old and New Testaments.

"The Sacred Scriptures of both the Old and the New Testaments, as well as ancient Tradition, show the role of the Mother of the Savior in the economy of salvation in an ever clearer light and draw attention to it" (*LG* 55).

All that is said about the iconography in this book follows the teachings and traditions of the Church in regard to the place of the Blessed Virgin Mary in the life of the Church.

This icon symbolizes the Church as evangelizer, illustrated by the way Mary stands boldly presenting Christ to all those who look upon her in their prayer. Her penetrating eyes invite us to enter the space of the redeeming love of Jesus Christ and to live our lives according to the spirit of the Gospel.

"In the interim just as the Mother of Jesus, glorified in body and soul in heaven, is the image and beginning of the Church as it is to be perfected in the world to come, so too does she shine forth on earth, until the day of the Lord shall come as a sign of...hope and solace to the people of God during its sojourn on earth" (*LG* 68).

In *Marialis Cultus,* Paul VI continues the development of devotion to Mary when he says: "The Blessed Virgin's role as Mother leads the People of God to turn with filial confidence to her who is ever ready to listen with a mother's affection and efficacious assistance. Thus the People of God have learned to call on her as the Consoler of the afflicted, the Health of the sick, and the Refuge of sinners, that they may find comfort in tribulation, relief in sickness and liberating strength in guilt" (*MC* 57).

> This icon continues to present themes of Mary found in the Scriptures and tradition.

Certainly this statement affirms the experience of so many people who come to Our Mother of Perpetual Help to ask her assistance in living the Christian life. How many over the years have found this haven of hope and healing? This refuge and blessing?

The Redemptorists continue to faithfully fulfill the mission given to them by Blessed Pope Pius IX of "making her known throughout the world." This book is just one of the many ways the Redemptorists continue the mission of spreading the message of the redeeming love of Jesus Christ present in the icon of Mother of Perpetual Help.

MOTHER OF PERPETUAL HELP, join YOUR PRAYERS TO OURS AS WE IMPLORE THE MERCY OF GOD IN OUR MANY NEEDS. FOR GOD WHO IS MIGHTY HAS DONE GREAT THINGS FOR YOU, AND HOLY IS HIS NAME. AMEN.

✳

PART III

Prayers and Exercises

Experiencing the Icon's Energy

We experience the powerful energy of an icon through our eyes. Looking into a holy icon, we experience the holy looking back at us. This is the contemplative experience of praying with icons.

Place the icon before you at eye level. When you pray with icons of Mary, open your Bible to the Gospel of Luke. Gently place your hands on the written word and slowly allow your eyes to gaze on the icon.

Do a simple, quiet reading of the icon, and then slowly close your eyes and become aware of the silence that surrounds you. Rest in this silence, letting distractions fade away. Stay in this silence for as long as you want.

When you wish to return to your current milieu, slowly open your eyes. As you return your gaze to the icon, read a passage from Luke. End the experience by gently reciting a Hail Mary.

Icons are more than religious art; they are passages into the world of mystery. In the many icons of Mary, we are influenced by her virtues and attitudes. We feel Mary's spirit—her faithfulness, her humility, and her pondering of the mysteries of God.

The Prayer of Gazing

Prayer is descending with the mind into the heart and standing in the presence of God. This is truly the practice of praying with icons. It is important that in whatever prayer position we use that we have the icon at eye level.

The prayer of gazing is a powerful form of contemplative prayer. Our eyes behold the beauty and glory of God present before us. As you begin your prayer of gazing, quiet yourself and become aware of your breathing. As distractions come into your mind, gently acknowledge them and let them go.

After a few minutes of silence, close your eyes and become aware of your desire to be with God at this moment. Ask God to help you let go of whatever may distance you from God's closeness.

Let your eyes make contact with the image. Go with whatever thoughts enter your mind about the icon. Usually they will lead to feelings and thoughts about the mystery of Christ. When distractions occur, let your gazing be the tool that brings you back to reflecting on the icon.

> Icons are more than religious art; they are passages into the world of mystery.

Close your eyes and try to retain a sense of the icon in your awareness. Then let it fade to a formless presence and remain in this silence as long as you wish.

Conclude your prayer time by praying the Our Father slowly in a low voice.

Chapter 11

Prayers and Exercises

Novena Prayers
to Our Mother of Perpetual Help

A novena is nine days or weeks of prayer. It is modeled on the nine days of prayer that the Blessed Virgin Mary and the apostles kept from the ascension to Pentecost (Acts 1:14). The word *novena* comes from the Latin word *novem*, meaning "nine." Those who make this novena are praying for special intentions and needs in their lives, asking Mary to pray with them for nine days.

> Ask God to help you let go
> of whatever may distance
> you from God's closeness.

In the name of the Father, the Son, and the Holy Spirit. Amen.

†

Mother of Perpetual Help, with the greatest confidence I come before your Holy Icon to implore your help. I confine, not in my merits or good works, but in the fidelity of Jesus to his promises and in your maternal assistance in my present need. You, O Mother, have seen the wounds of the Redeemer and his bloodshed upon the cross for our salvation. It was your dying Son who gave you to us as a Mother. O Mother of Perpetual Help, for the sake of the painful passion and death of your divine Son, for the sake of the indescribable suffering of your own heart, I plead with you to obtain from the Lord this favor, which I earnestly seek, and of which I have such great need. (Here, express your petition.) You know, Mother of God, how much Jesus wishes to bestow upon all of us the benefits of his redemption. Mother of God of Perpetual Help, we are ever grateful for all gifts received from God through your assistance. Rejoice, O Virgin Mary, Rejoice Full of Grace. O Mary, our Mother, we thank you for your "yes" to God to become his Mother. Join your prayers to ours as we implore the mercy of God in our needs.

Pray a Hail Mary

Scripture:

Exult greatly, O daughter Zion! Shout for joy, O daughter Jerusalem! Behold: your king is coming to you, a just savior is he, Humble, and riding on a donkey, on a colt, the foal of a donkey (Zechariah 9:9).

Silent Reflection

Acclamation:

It is truly right to bless you, O God-bearing one, as the ever blessed and immaculate Mother of our God. More honorable than the cherubim and by far more glorious than the seraphim; ever a virgin, you gave birth to God the Word, O true Mother of God, we magnify you.

Litany:

Holy Mary, pray for us.
Mother of Jesus, pray for us.
Tabernacle of the Holy Spirit, pray for us.
Mother of the poor, pray for us.
Health of the sick, pray for us.
Consolation of the suffering, pray for us.
Mother of God of Perpetual Help, pray for us.

Acclamation:

O pure and holy Virgin Mary, the highest heavens cannot contain God, whom you carried in your womb. Blessed are you among women, and blessed is the fruit of your womb.

Let Us Pray:

All powerful and merciful Lord, you gave us the icon of the Mother of your Son to venerate under the title of Our Mother of Perpetual Help. Graciously grant that in all the difficulties of our lives we may be assisted by the continuous protection of the Virgin Mary and obtain the reward of eternal redemption. You live and reign forever and ever. Amen.

An Akathist Hymn in Honor of the Mother of Perpetual Help

A Prayer to the Blessed Virgin Mary in the Byzantine Tradition by Servant of God Fr. Roman Bachtalowsky, CSsR

The Akathist prayer is reproduced here with the permission of the Yorkton Province of the Redemptorists.

Kondak I

Glorious Queen and source of God's grace, we the faithful come before your famous icon, from which you continuously dispense your graces. Keep under your perpetual protection your spiritual children who have dedicated their lives to you and sing in your honor: Rejoice, O Full of Grace, our Hope.

Ikos I

O Full of Grace, many angels stand before your glorious throne and continuously sing: Rejoice! For they cannot otherwise exalt you nor admire your beauty. We who have gathered before your icon raise our eyes to heaven and together with the angels say:

Rejoice, O Full of Grace, the Lord is with you.

Rejoice, O Source of heavenly treasures.

Rejoice, O Star, shining over the whole earth.

Rejoice, O Fountain of mercy, which can never be exhausted.

Rejoice, O Queen and Mother of God's elect.

Rejoice, O Land, flowing with honey which nourishes many.

Rejoice, O Foretold Tree, which covers us all with its shadow.

Rejoice, O Fruitful Olive Tree, fragrant like Lebanon.

Rejoice, for your hands, like those of Moses, are always raised to pray for us.

Rejoice, for you can obtain everything from God by your prayers.

Rejoice, O Hope for all generations.

Rejoice, O Cause of our joy.

Rejoice, O Full of Grace, our hope!

Кондак 2

A merchant of Crete knew of your icon, this precious jewel, for it was beautiful and famous for its miracles. He took it from the church, hid it in his vessel and set out for sea. O Most Pure One, you are our most precious treasure, therefore we go through the sea of life toward a happy eternity, our heavenly City, singing: Alleluia!

Ікоs 2

We see the wisdom of God's providence which is beyond our understanding. Immaculate Virgin, wishing to save your icon from the pagans, God transferred it to Rome, so that all nations could glorify it. He wished through your prayers, Mother of God, to dispense bountiful graces and show mercy to his people, for by touching it as if it were the biblical Ark, we find not death, but life. Mother of God, you are truly a spiritual Ark, for you carried in your hands not the tablets of the covenant nor the staff budded forth or the golden urn, but Christ, the unfading Flower and Lawmaker. Pray to Him for those who sing to you:

Rejoice, O Sacred Ark of the New Testament.

Rejoice, O reliable Weapon, for you overcome the enemy armies.

Rejoice, O Leader through the desert of life.

Rejoice, O Jesse's Tree on which a divine Flower has blossomed.

Rejoice, O Fruitful Vine, whose seed grows up on the stones of indifference.

Rejoice, for the spirit of counsel and fortitude has rested upon you.

Rejoice, O Tablet of God's mercy.

Rejoice, O Manna, sweeter than honey.

Rejoice, O Lampstand of seven branches that enlightens all.

Rejoice, O Model created in the image of the uncreated reflection of the Father.

Rejoice, O Life-giving Ray of eternal life.

Rejoice, O Holy Unshakable Throne of Christ the King.

Rejoice, O Full of Grace, our Hope!

Kондак 3

Mother of God, the power of the Most High God manifests itself in every place where your precious icon is devoutly honored. Here the sick regain their health, the suffering receive comfort, and those who dwell in darkness obtain the spiritual sight of the soul and body. For you attract all with your goodness that you may lead them to your heart and thus turn them toward Christ, the never-setting Sun, when they sing: Alleluia!

Ikos 3

Mother of God, we have a precious jewel, your icon which came to us from the East. We bow before you as before a bright star and announcer of God's day for where you appear, salvation comes to those who sing to you:

Rejoice, O Unguarded Gate of paradise.

Rejoice, O Unlocked Treasure, from which all can profit.

Rejoice, O Source of the living Water, ever-streaming.

Rejoice, O Dew which falls upon the mount of Zion.

Rejoice, O Sweet Potion for thirsty souls.

Rejoice, for you gave the bread of fortitude to the hungry which strengthens people.

Rejoice, O strong Bulwark Wall of God's city which embraces the whole world.

Rejoice, O House of the Lord which is built on a hilltop.

Rejoice, O Fruitful Hill upon which God made His Home.

Rejoice, O Altar of Christ the King.

Rejoice, O Chamber of glory which never fades away.

Rejoice, O Full of Grace, our Hope!

Rejoice, O Full of Grace, our Hope!

Kondak 4

The remorse of conscience tortured the merchant of Crete when he found himself on his deathbed, until he had repented and commissioned his friend to return your icon to a church. Then he placed himself under your protection and with your help completed his earthly life and reached the peaceful, eternal haven, singing: Alleluia!

Ikos 4

Hearing about the great miracle by which you moved the heart of the unrepenting merchant, the people came with their bishops and priests, and carrying countless candles took your icon to the church, singing:

Rejoice, O Mary, our Gracious Queen.

Rejoice, O Holy and merciful Mother of God.

Rejoice, O Virgin of all virgins the most illustrious.

Rejoice, O enclosed Garden of the Lord.

Rejoice, O Sealed Fountain of God.

Rejoice, O Well of the Living Water.

Rejoice, O Fragrant Lily filling all with its aroma.

Rejoice, O most beautiful Chosen One of God.

Rejoice, O Holy of the Holiest.

Rejoice, filled with Divine Glory.

Rejoice, for you are the glory and charm of all generations.

Rejoice, O Full of Grace, our hope.

Rejoice, O Full of Grace, our hope!

Кондак 5

When you saw the blood and spear which was to pierce the
Heart of your Son as well as the gall and the cross in the hands
of the angels, you noticed in the wondrous vision that He would
be the hope of all nations. Thus you soul was stricken by a deadly
fear. Embracing your Child, you wept bitterly saying: How can
I offer you in sacrifice, my Son, who are so comely and the most
beautiful of all the sons of men? How can I go through all your
sufferings, O my gracious Light? How will I heal the wounds of
my soul that your wounds will inflict upon it? For the sake of the
salvation of the world, however, do whatever you wish with your
handmaid, who sings: Alleluia!

İkos 5

All-suffering Mother, all the countries of the earth have seen your
compassion toward your Son who is represented on this icon.
They looked at it and wondered that you delivered as a ransom
your Christ who is beyond all price so that you may deliver your
spiritual children from the slavery of hell. With what hymn of
praise may I sing about your love? How may I exalt your greatness
in your sufferings? Which fragrant spiritual flowers may I place
on your painful path? Wherefore as a child I will only sing to you:

Rejoice, O Queen and Mother.

Rejoice, O Immaculate Eve.

Rejoice, O loving Mother.

Rejoice, You whose love is beyond expression and destruction.

Rejoice, O Treasure of my heart.

Rejoice, O Sweetness of my soul.

Rejoice, for in your painful sufferings you gave us spiritual birth
at the cross.

Rejoice, because you sacrificed everything for the sake of your
spiritual children.

Rejoice, for you accepted the cross during the angelic visitation.

Rejoice, for you were the first to drink from the bitter chalice of
Christ throughout your whole life.

Rejoice, O Rachel of the New Testament for you are weeping for your children killed by the hellish enemy.

Rejoice, O fiery Love which could not be extinguished even by the greatest of sufferings.

Rejoice, O Full of Grace, our Hope!

Kοπdak 6

Most Holy Mother of God, you have chosen for yourself the divinely inspired preachers of redemption to guard your icon. Following in the footsteps of their founder, Alphonsus, they preach your greatness throughout the whole world, teaching everyone to glorify you as a mediatrix of grace and through you they exalt God, exclaiming: Alleluia.

İkos 6

Your miraculous icon shines throughout the whole world and is honored everywhere, gathering your children, dispersed throughout the world, brothers and sisters divided among themselves, so that, like so many shining stars, they may enter the kingdom of Christ and sing:

Rejoice, O Leader of those who wander in darkness.

Rejoice, O Deliverer of those whom darkness has imprisoned.

Rejoice, O Woman custodian of Christ's Vineyard.

Rejoice, of all women the most beautiful.

Rejoice, for you are the guardian of the fold of your Son.

Rejoice, O Queen sitting at the right hand of your Son and Lord.

Rejoice, O Lady vested in a golden robe.

Rejoice, adorned with divine beauty.

Rejoice, for you are glorified from generation to generation.

Rejoice, O Tree of Life always fruitful and filled with the Holy Spirit.

Rejoice, O Morning Star, announcing the Sun.

Rejoice, O Full of Grace, our Hope!

Kοɴdaк 7

Wishing to save the whole world, He that became Mediator for all chose you as His suffering companion and intercessor for our salvation. He left everything to you during His Passion on the cross and made you the Mother of us all who believe in Him and glorify Him, saying: Alleluia!

Ìκos 7

God's wisdom planted the Church as a new garden for itself and made it a source of the living water. You came forth from it and now you water with grace the whole earth, O Full of Grace. The luxuriant spiritual vineyards grow, the flowers of piety blossom, the lilies of virginity and the myrrh of martyrdom flourish. Inspired by the Holy Spirit, they all sing to you:

Rejoice, resplendent, life-creating Flower.

Rejoice, for you transform the desertlike hearts into magnificent gardens.

Rejoice, O Virgin Field for you nurture the flowers of chastity.

Rejoice, O Vine of Christ's Vineyard which yields clusters of martyrs.

Rejoice, O Water of Siloam which cures the blind of heart.

Rejoice, for you purify the offerings soiled by the passions.

Rejoice, O Pool and wash me like a lamb destined for sacrifice.

Rejoice, O Dove which announces the New Earth.

Rejoice, O Rainbow which reminds us of the eternal covenant.

Rejoice, O New Testament Ruth for you collect the abandoned ears of corn.

Rejoice, O Tree whose leaves cure all nations.

Rejoice, O Gate of the new Jerusalem which is open day and night.

Rejoice, O Full of Grace, our Hope!

Kondak 8

It is a wondrous mystery, beyond our understanding, O Lord, our God, how can you, O God, do what a creature, your most Blessed Mother wills of You? You have, however, made known your will to her in such a way that she may ask only for things that agree with Your Will, lead all on the path of your Commandments and distribute our gifts according to your providence to those who sing: Alleluia!

Ikos 8

Most Blessed Virgin Mary, you can do everything both in heaven and on earth. You can convert sinners and heal the sick. Being a handmaid of the Lord, you humbled yourself more than anyone else, but with your prayers you surpass all angelic Powers and Dominions. You have so wounded with love the Heart of Your Son that He can never refuse your petitions. Thus our eyes are always turned to you, O Queen Mother, until you bestow your abundant graces on us who sing to you:

Rejoice, O Virgin that prays unceasingly for us.

Rejoice, O Altar upon which the incense is always burning.

Rejoice, O Resplendent Crown of Christ's Church.

Rejoice, O Chalice of Heavenly Joy.

Rejoice, O Holy Mountain from which God speaks to His people.

Rejoice, O Table of Divine Sweetness.

Rejoice, O Garden of the Flowerbeds of the Holy Spirit.

Rejoice, for with your word you united heaven and earth in Christ.

Rejoice, for a new creation appeared through your prayers.

Rejoice, O Fountain of mercy for poor sinners.

Rejoice, for you helped the repentant sinners to reach the thrones of the Seraphim.

Rejoice, for you have made holy the whole world with your mercy.

Rejoice, O Full of Grace, our Hope!

Копдак 9

O ever-praised One, all nations waited for you because you were promised since time immemorial. You were destined to become the Immaculate Mother of the Savior, the beginning and source of all miracles. When you finally appeared, the people of God rejoiced, singing: Alleluia!

Íkos 9

Even the most eloquent orators are unable to praise you fully for the miracles you perform for your servants that come before your icon. Everyone—the poor, the suffering and the forsaken—knows that though a mother may forsake her own children, you, O ever-gracious, will never forget your spiritual children who cry out to you:

Rejoice, O loving Mother of orphans.

Rejoice, O Gracious Refuse for those who cannot find shelter.

Rejoice, O brilliant Light which helps the blind regain their sight.

Rejoice, O Holy Oil which heals the wounds of hearts.

Rejoice, O Hope of despairing sinners.

Rejoice, for you calm the worried.

Rejoice, O Mother of our Benefactor Christ.

Rejoice, for you enrich us with all kinds of gifts.

Rejoice, for your hands always bless and heal people.

Rejoice, O Queen who reigns by goodness, not by violence.

Rejoice, for you resemble the wind of paradise which dries the tears of the people.

Rejoice, for you fill all with heavenly joy.

Rejoice, O Full of Grace, our Hope!

Kондаk 10

O Good Lord, as once you gave a rainbow to your servants, so now you present the icon of Your Mother to those who perish in the desert of life. If we come to it with confidence, we will receive the miraculous potion of your abundant mercy, singing: Alleluia.

İkos 10

Good Lady, in you we find an immovable Wall and a true Tower of defense for all, whom God made capable of a strenuous fight against the prince of darkness, Satan. Vested in breastplates of faith, they courageously resist the attacks of your enemies, signing the victorious hymn:

Rejoice, O Strong Woman who resembles the regiments ready for battle.

Rejoice, O Woman who crushed the serpent's head.

Rejoice, for you inspired courage in Christ's Army.

Rejoice, O Sacred Key that guards the temple of priestly holiness.

Rejoice, O Helper and Leader of the pastors of souls.

Rejoice, O strength of those who suffer for the Christian faith.

Rejoice, O Secure Shelter from violent temptations.

Rejoice, Who strengthens kingdoms and nations.

Rejoice, O Chosen Captain.

Rejoice, for you deliver your people from foreign violence.

Rejoice, O Defender of the helpless.

Rejoice, O Full of Grace, our Hope.

Rejoice, O Full of Grace, our Hope!

Kondak II

With love we will sing the hymn first sung by the Archangel when he announced the coming of Emmanuel and brought joy to the world, for with it we overcome our enemies and secure your perpetual help and heavenly joy, for because of you, God dwells with us. This is why we exclaim: Alleluia!

Ikos II

Gracious, Never-setting Sun of my poor soul in this vale of tears, where labors, sufferings, struggles against the passions, attacks and ambushes of the infernal enemies endeavor to destroy my soul! Now will I complete my difficult journey if you do not strengthen me with your prayers and perpetual help and do not enlighten me, who exclaims to you:

Rejoice, O Gracious Light of those who have blinded themselves by their sins.

Rejoice, O Star leading to the sovereign King, Christ.

Rejoice, O cloudy Pillar in the desert of life.

Rejoice, O Dew of my thirsty soul.

Rejoice, O Calm Haven among stormy passions.

Rejoice, O Leader on the journey of life.

Rejoice, O Healer of wounds, inflicted by life.

Rejoice, for you have broken my sinful chains.

Rejoice, O Full of Grace, our Hope!

Koпdak 12

My ever-praised Queen, obtain for me the grace to keep my soul pure all my life, for Christ has washed it with his blood. I entrust my salvation to you and therefore I firmly hope that you will be my lighted lamp at the frightful moment of my battle before death and that you will meet me with a lighted candle to light the last steps of my journey and lead me to God, the joy of my youthful years. My soul will eternally rejoice in heaven and exalt you forever with festive hymns, singing: Alleluia!

İkos 12

Singing and constantly glorifying you with indescribable hymns, the Cherubim and the Seraphim, together with the countless angels and saints who are all ages are rejoicing in heaven offer you as so many wreaths of prayers of your servants who ask for your help from all over the world. They watch your face, shining like the sun, and wait only for your command to help save all those who sing to you:

Rejoice, O prayerful Lady of the world.

Rejoice, O Shining Sun which enlightens the heavens and the universe.

Rejoice, O head of the Cherubim.

Rejoice, O mysterious Treasure of God's Providence.

Rejoice, O Instrument of the Holy Spirit.

Rejoice, O head of all creation, humbled at first and now exalted above the Seraphim.

Rejoice, O Handmaid of the Lord who always does the Will of God.

Rejoice, O Full of Grace, our Hope!

Kondak 13

O Mother of the whole world, worthy of all praise! You begot Christ in our souls. Accept from us, your spiritual children, this earnest prayer and keep in the love for your Son all of us who have submitted to the Will of God. Lead us to everlasting glory in heaven as we sing in your honor: Alleluia!

Prayer to the Mother of Perpetual Help

Most pure Mother of God, Immaculate Virgin, Queen of the World, Intercessor of Christians, refuge and hope of sinners, I, the most miserable of all, kneel before your icon. I humbly bow to you, O my ever-praised Queen, I wholeheartedly thank you for all the graces which you have so abundantly bestowed on me. But most of all, I thank you for saving me from the infernal tortures which I have so many times deserved.

I love you, O my Queen, and for the sake of this love I promise to serve you forever and do whatever I can that others may also serve, honor, and love you. O Merciful Mother, after God you are my hope and cause of my salvation. Accept me, your servant, under your mighty Protection. You can obtain everything from God. Pray to Him to deliver me from all temptations and dangers, or at least help me to overcome them. Obtain also for me the virtues of a strong faith, firm hope, and true, nonhypocritical love. Be with me especially at the last moment of my earthly life.

My gracious Lady, it is not through my prayers but rather through your love for God that I implore you. Do not forsake me until you see me in heaven, where I will forever praise and thank you in the Kingdom of Your Son, to whom, together with His Eternal Father and the Holy Good and Life-creating Spirit, belong all glory, honor, and adoration, now and always and forever. Amen.

PART IV

The History of the Icon and Its Restoration

The History of the Icon

The following is reprinted with the permission of the Redemptorists. It originally appeared on the CSsR website.

T here is a tradition from the sixteenth century that tells us about a merchant from the isle of Crete who stole a miraculous picture from one of its churches. He hid it among his wares and set out westward. It was only through Divine Providence that he survived a wild tempest and landed on solid ground. After about a year, he arrived in Rome with his stolen picture.

It was there that he became mortally ill and looked for a friend to care for him. At his hour of death, he revealed his secret of the picture and begged his friend to return it to a church. His friend promised to fulfill this wish, but because his wife did not want to relinquish such a beautiful treasure, the friend also died without fulfilling the promise.

At last, the Blessed Virgin appeared to the six-year-old daughter of this Roman family and told her to tell her mother and grandmother that the picture of Holy Mary of Perpetual Help should be placed in the Church of St. Matthew the Apostle, located between the basilicas of St. Mary Major and St. John Lateran.

The tradition relates how, after many doubts and difficulties, "the mother obeyed and after consulting with the clergy in charge of the church, the picture of the Virgin was placed in St. Matthew's, on the 27th of March, 1499." There it would be venerated during the next 300 years. Thus began the second stage of the history of the icon, and devotion to Our Mother of Perpetual Help began to spread throughout the city of Rome.

Three Centuries in the Church of St. Matthew
Saint Matthew's Church was not grand but it possessed an enormous treasure that attracted the faithful: the icon of Our Mother of Perpetual Help. From 1739 to 1798, the church and adjacent monastery were under the care of the Irish Augustinians who had been unjustly exiled from their country and used the monastery as a formation center for their Roman Province. The young students found an asylum of peace in the presence of the Virgin of Perpetual Help while they prepared themselves for priesthood, the apostolate and martyrdom.

In 1798, war raged in Rome, and the monastery and church were almost totally destroyed. Several Augustinians remained there for a few more years, but eventually they, too, had to leave. Some returned to Ireland, others to new foundations in America, while the majority moved to a nearby monastery. This last group brought with them the picture of Our Lady of Perpetual Help. Thus began the third stage of her history, the "Hidden Years."

In 1819, the Irish Augustinians moved to the Church of St. Mary in Posterula, near the Umberto I bridge that crosses the Tiber River. With them went the Virgin of St. Matthew's. But as Our Lady of Grace was already venerated in this church, the newly arrived picture was placed in a private chapel in the monastery where it remained, all but forgotten, but for Brother Augustine Orsetti, one of the original young friars from St. Matthew's.

The Old Religious and the Young Altar Boy
The years passed, and it seemed that the picture that had been saved from the war that destroyed St. Matthew's Church was about to be lost in oblivion.

A young altar boy named Michael Marchi often visited the Church of Sancta Maria in Posterula and became friends with Brother Augustine. Much later, as Father Michael, he would write:

"This good brother used to tell me with a certain air of mystery and anxiety, especially during the years 1850 and 1851, these precise words. 'Make sure you know, my son, that the image of the Virgin of St. Matthew is upstairs in the chapel: Don't ever forget it....Do you understand? It is a miraculous picture.' At that time the brother was almost totally blind.

"What I can say about the venerable picture of the Virgin of St. Matthew, also called Perpetual Help, is that from my childhood until I entered the Congregation (of the Redemptorists) I had always seen it above the altar of the house chapel of the Augustinian Fathers of the Irish Province at St. Mary in Posterula....There was no devotion to it, no decorations, not even a lamp to acknowledge its presence....It remained covered with dust and practically abandoned. Many were the times, when I served Mass there, that I would stare at it with great attention."

Brother Augustine died in 1853 at the venerable age of eighty-six without seeing fulfilled his desire that the Virgin of Perpetual Help be once again exposed for public veneration. His prayers and boundless confidence in the Virgin Mary seemed to have gone unanswered.

The Rediscovery of the Icon
In January of 1855, the Redemptorist Missionaries purchased Villa Caserta in Rome, converting it into the general house for their missionary congregation that had spread to western Europe and North America. On this same property along the Via Merulana, were the ruins of the Church and Monastery of St. Matthew. Without realizing it at the time, they had acquired the land that, many years previously, had been chosen by the Virgin as her sanctuary between St. Mary Major and St. John Lateran.

Four months later, construction was begun on a church in honor of the Most Holy Redeemer and dedicated to St. Alphonsus Liguori, founder of the Congregation. On December 24, 1855, a group of young men began their novitiate in the new house. One of them was Michael Marchi.

The Redemptorists were extremely interested in the history of their new property. But more so, when on February 7, 1863, they were puzzled by the questioning from a sermon given by the famous Jesuit preacher, Father Francesco Blosi, about an icon of Mary that "had been in the Church of St. Matthew on Via Merulana and was known as the Virgin of St. Matthew, or more correctly as the Virgin of Perpetual Help."

On another occasion, the chronicler of the Redemptorist community, "examining some authors who had written about Roman antiquities, found references made to the Church of St. Matthew. Among them there was a particular citation mentioning that in the church (which had been situated within the garden area of the community) there had been an ancient icon of the Mother of God that enjoyed 'great veneration and fame for its miracles.'" Then, "having told all this to the community, a dialogue began as to where they could locate the picture. Father Marchi remembered all that he had heard from old Brother Augustine Orsetti and told his confreres that he had often seen the icon and knew very well where it could be found."

The Reception of the Icon by the Redemptorists
With this new information, interest grew among the Redemptorists to know more about the icon and to retrieve it for their church. The Superior General, Father Nicholas Mauron, presented a letter to Pope Pius IX in which he petitioned the Holy See to grant them the icon of Perpetual Help and that it be placed in the newly built Church of the Most Holy Redeemer and St. Alphonsus, which was located near the site where the old Church of St. Matthew had stood. The Pope granted the request and on the back of the petition, in his own handwriting he noted:

"December 11, 1865: The Cardinal Prefect of Propaganda will call the Superior of the community of Sancta Maria in Posterula and will tell him that it is Our desire that the image of Most Holy Mary, referred to in this petition, be again placed between Saint John and St. Mary Major; the Redemptorists shall replace it with another adequate picture."

According to tradition, this was when Pope Pius IX told the

Redemptorist Superior General: "Make Her known throughout the world!" In January 1866, Fathers Michael Marchi and Ernest Bresciani went to St. Mary's in Posterula to receive the picture from the Augustinians.

Then began the process of cleaning and retouching the icon. The task was entrusted to the Polish artist, Leopold Nowotny. Finally, on April 26th, 1866, the image was again presented for public veneration in the Church of St. Alphonsus on the Via Merulana.

With this event, the fourth stage of her history began: the spread of the icon throughout the world.

The Latest Restoration of the Icon
In 1990, the picture of Our Mother of Perpetual Help was taken down from above the main altar to satisfy the many requests for new photographs of the icon. It was then that the serious state of deterioration of the image was discovered; the wood, as well as the paint, had suffered from environmental changes and prior attempts at restoration. The General Government of the Redemptorists decided to contract the technical services of the Vatican Museum to bring about a general restoration of the icon that would deal with the cracks and fungus that threatened irreparable damage.

The first part of the restoration consisted of a series of X-rays, infrared images, qualitative and quantitative analyses of the paint, and other infra-red and ultraviolet tests. The results of these analyses, especially a carbon-14 test, indicated that the wood of the icon of Perpetual Help could safely be dated from the years 1325–1480.

The second stage of the restoration consisted of the physical work of filling the cracks and perforations in the wood, cleaning the paint and retouching the affected sections, strengthening the structure that sustains the icon, etc. This physical intervention was limited to the absolute minimum because all restorative work, somewhat like bodily surgery, always provokes some trauma. An artistic analysis situated the pigmentation of the paint at a later date (after the seventeenth century); this would explain why the icon offers a synthesis of Oriental and Occidental elements, especially in its facial aspects.

Conclusion

I once heard an ancient story about St. Andrew that I believe is a wonderful ending for this book on the icon of Our Mother of Perpetual Help. It sums up in a simple fable the experience of the Holy Mother of God of Perpetual Help in the lives of countless people.

After his martyrdom, St. Andrew arrives in heaven after living on earth with a great love for the cross of Christ and the Mother of God, who witnesses the suffering and death of her Son on the cross.

Being admitted to the realm of heaven, he began searching for the Mother of God. "Where is she?" St. Andrew asked the angel who was guiding him through heaven. "She's not here," the angel replied. "She is walking on earth among the suffering masses, drying the tears of her weeping children."

Rejoice, Virgin Mary! Rejoice, Full of Grace!